Secrets

of

Success

ONE FOR EACH DAY
OF THE MONTH

D1449303

J. DONALD WALTERS

Hardbound Edition
First Printing 1993

ISBN 1-56589-031-0

PRINTED IN HONG KONG

Crystal Clarity
PUBLISHERS

14618 Tyler Foote Road, Nevada City, CA 95959
1 (800) 424-1055

seed thought is offered for every day of the month. Begin a day at the appropriate date. Repeat the saying several times: first out loud, then softly, then in a whisper, and then only mentally. With each repetition, allow the words to become absorbed ever more deeply into your subconscious. Thus, gradually, you will acquire as complete an understanding as one might gain from a year's course in the subject. At this point, indeed, the truths set forth here will have become your own.

Keep the book open at the pertinent page throughout the day. Refer to it occasionally during moments of leisure. Relate the saying as often as possible to real situations in your life.

Then at night, before you go to bed, repeat the thought several times more. While falling asleep, carry the words into your subconscious, absorbing their positive influence into your whole being. Let it become thereby an integral part of your normal consciousness.

Day 1

The Secret of

SUCCESS

is enjoying,

never bemoaning,

whatever effort

a work requires.

Day 2

The

Secret of Success

is doing things not merely

because they are popular,

but because you

deeply believe

in them.

The Secret of Success
is working with
things as they are,
not with the way
you wish they were
or think they ought to be.

Day 3

The Secret of

Su   c

Day 4

c e s s

is non-attachment to results;

doing your best at the moment,

and letting the results

take care of themselves.

Day 5

The

Secret of Success

is

Enthusiasm!

—•◆•—

Without it,

nothing worthwhile

was ever achieved.

Day 6

The Secret of

SUCCESS

is asking yourself always,

not, "What do I want

to see happen?" but rather,

"What is trying to happen here?"

THE SECRET OF

Success

IS SEEING YOUR WORK

PRIMARILY AS A SERVICE

TO OTHERS, AND NOT AS

A MEANS OF PERSONAL GAIN.

Day

8

The Secret of Success

■

is blaming no one

when things go wrong,

but doing whatever you can

to improve matters.

DAY 9

THE SECRET OF Success

IS BEING CRYSTAL CLEAR

AS TO YOUR PURPOSE

AND DIRECTIONS,

AND HAVING THE COURAGE

TO ACT ACCORDINGLY.

Day 10

The Secret of Success

is

*W*elcoming

as opportunities

whatever obstacles

confront you.

Day Eleven

The Secret of

SUCCESS

is seeing every setback

as a steppingstone

to ultimate achievement.

Day 12

The
Secret of
SUCCESS

is developing your will power,

by setting yourself

increasingly difficult goals,

and persevering until

each of them

has been achieved.

DAY 13

THE SECRET

OF SUCCESS IS

EING MORE

ENERGY-ORIENTED

THAN GOAL-ORIENTED;

SEEING LIFE IN TERMS

OF CONSTANT PROGRESS,

NOT OF PRE-ESTABLISHED ENDS.

$_{Day}$ **14**

The Secret of

Success

is daring to
step outside the
boundaries of
conventional
wisdom.

Day 15

The Secret
of Success

is the ability

to concentrate

one-pointedly

on whatever task

you set yourself.

The Secret of

Success

is viewing every day

as a fresh beginning,

bright with promise,

and never defining

yourself in terms of

past accomplishments.

Day Sixteen

The secret of success

is not limiting your self-identity

to present realities,

but expanding it to include

your highest potentials.

Day 17

Day

18

The

Secret of

SUCCESS

is willingness

to re-evaluate

your first principles.

The secret of success
is ensuring that the outcome
of everything you do
be harmonious,
by acting always with
a positive, harmonious attitude.

Day

19

Day Twenty

The Secret of Success

is asking yourself

in anything you do, not merely,

"What would people like to have?"

but, "What would I feel happy

giving them?"

THE **S**ECRET OF SUCCESS

IS OPENNESS TO THE *Truth,*

NO MATTER BY WHOM IT IS UTTERED.

DAY 21

The Secret

of Success

is a preference

for the truth

over mere opinion —

even if the opinion

be your own.

Day Twenty-two

The Secret

of

Suc

Day 23

c e s s

is consulting your inner

feeling before making decisions;

never doing a thing,

whatever Reason tells you,

unless your heart concurs.

Day 24

The Secret of Success

is never making emotional

decisions, but maintaining

your heart's feeling in a calm

state of reason.

The Secret of Success

⊞

is being solution-oriented,

not problem-oriented,

and having faith that,

for every problem,

an inherent solution exists.

Day 25

THE SECRET OF SUCCESS

IS BEING *Grateful*

FOR WHAT YOU HAVE,

HOWEVER LITTLE,

AND NOT RESENTING LIFE

FOR WHAT IT HASN'T GIVEN YOU.

THE SECRET OF SUCCESS
IS NOT MAKING EXCUSES
FOR YOURSELF WHEN
THINGS GO WRONG,
BUT REFLECTING THAT
GOD ALONE IS INFALLIBLE.

DAY TWENTY-SEVEN

Day 28

The Secret of

S U C C E S S

—◦❦◦—

is understanding that

you are the final measure

of everything you accomplish.

For that work alone is noble

which ennobles its creator.

DAY 29

The Secret of Success

IS MEETING CHALLENGES

BY REMAINING CALMLY

CENTERED WITHIN,

AND SEEKING STRENGTH

AND GUIDANCE INTUITIVELY,

IN YOUR INNER SELF.

The Secret of Success

is

Attuning

your limited, human will

to the infinite divine will.

Day 30

Day

31

The secret of success

is *Humility*,

realizing that pride

is the death of wisdom,

and the paralysis of

every worthwhile endeavor.

Other Books by J. Donald Walters

Hardbound

SECRETS OF HAPPINESS $5.95

SECRETS OF FRIENDSHIP $5.95

SECRETS OF INNER PEACE $5.95

SECRETS OF LOVE $5.95

Soft Cover

AFFIRMATIONS FOR SELF-HEALING This inspirational book offers insights into 52 different qualities such as willpower, forgiveness, and openness, through the use of affirmations and prayer. $7.95

MONEY MAGNETISM: *How to Attract What You Need When You Need It* This book offers fresh, new insights on proven ways of increasing money magnetism without making it a burden on one's peace of mind. $7.95

THE ART OF SUPPORTIVE LEADERSHIP An invaluable tool for anyone in a position of responsibility who views management in terms of shared accomplishment rather than personal advancement. $7.95

Order Form

Use this order form and receive a **20% discount** on this purchase.
Please fill out opposite side of this form to complete your order.

QUANTITY	ITEM	PRICE
_____	_____	_____
_____	_____	_____
_____	_____	_____
_____	_____	_____
_____	_____	_____

Shipping and Handling

Up to $10.00 = $3.00
$10.01 to $20.00 = $4.00
$20.01 to $45.00 = $5.00
$45.01 to $55.00 = $6.00
$55.01 to $65.00 = $7.00
$65.01 to $80.00 = $8.00
Over $80.00 = 10% of total

Subtotal _____

20% discount _____

7.25% sales tax in
California _____

Shipping and Handling
(See chart to left) _____

☐ I love this book! Please send me
your free catalogue of over 300
books, tapes, and videos.

TOTAL _____

Order Form *(continued)*

Please send check or money order and this form to Crystal Clarity, Publishers, 14618 Tyler Foote Road, Nevada City, CA 95959, or call toll free 1 (800) 424-1055.

Name ————————————————————————

Address ————————————————————————

City ————————————————————————

State ———————————— Zip ————————

Telephone ————————————————————

Please charge to my credit card: ☐ Visa ☐ MasterCharge

Credit card # ————————————————————

Exp. date ————————————————————